The L

of

Love

Quotes from the book

Take Control of Your Spacecraft and Fly Back to Love

A Manual and Guidebook for Life's Journey

By Keith Higgs

ISBN: Paperback 978-1-9997319-0-8
eBook 978-1-9997319-1-5

Rev. date 4/06/17 Ing

To order additional copies of this book contact:
Awake Your Dreams Books
+44 1799 610600
www.TheLittleBookofLove.info
orders@TheLittleBookofLove.info
or purchase through www.FlyBacktoLove.com

CONTENTS

♥♥♥♥♥♥♥♥♥

Section 2. Some Guidelines for Flight and Maintenance

Section 3.Taking Control

Section 4. Flying in Style

Section 5. Fly Back to Love

Introduction

♥♥♥♥♥♥♥♥♥

When we enter this life, we step into a world of forgetfulness, a world where the past is nothing but a concealed memory. We slowly develop an understanding of this new world and learn how to interact with the amazing vehicle, created by us for this journey. I liken it to a spacecraft, as it is perfectly fitted to fly us through this new life.

It is an amazing craft. There are trillions of cells working together, which produce a living vehicle for us to travel in. Our task is to learn to control and pilot this craft, on an amazing journey of discovery, learning and experience—back to the realm we came from—Love. We are at core, the essence of that Love—Pure Energy.

Now for our welfare, the craft has been given an autopilot capable of running itself and looking after its millions of complex manoeuvres. These control movement and even the decisions needed to control actions and emotions. Within this, lies both the blessing and the problem. Much of that early information and instruction was input a long time ago and may have served us well then, but as we evolve and grow, just like our computers need a new operating system —the craft continually needs to be reprogrammed for new ages and the ever growing, learning, new being, that is now piloting this earthly vehicle.

It is one of our challenges on this voyage of life, to come to an understanding of how this works. Then we need to take control of our vehicle, rather than letting its old programs and outmoded ideas, decisions and beliefs continue to shape our life and reality.

My book “Take Control of Your Spacecraft and Fly Back to Love - a Manual and Guidebook for Life's Journey.” was designed to share these ideas and especially help our understanding, and give some tools and signposts to assist on this journey Back to Love.

This Little book of Love is the heart and essence of that book. It is a collection of its most inspiring and powerful quotations. It’s easy and quick to read, and if assimilated, I believe contains many empowering, Love speeding, valuable ideas to assist us on our journeys.

You can read it through, or occasionally just open the book to see which quote Spirit leads you to, or dig through the index, researching subjects that speak to you. One of the best ways may be to take a quote and reread or meditate on it for a day or so. If it feels good and fits, then let it assimilate into your belief systems and autopilot. Then it can truly serve you. If not, find other ideas from the book or the multitude of sources available. I feel there are only a few absolute truths. Most of the things we consider truth are just ideas we have chosen to be our beliefs. These are the thoughts we have repeated over and over until they became our values and core programs. Be sure all the beliefs you hold dearly continue to serve you today, and especially are based on the only truth and one Law, that is to Love.

Best wishes on your journey.

Keith Higgs

Driving Your Vehicle What Is in Control?

I discovered that
some of the systems,
especially guidance
and direction,
have been hijacked
and reprogrammed
by others,
rather than
by the maker.

Some of the gauges have
also got stuck in flight,
limiting levels of happiness,
wealth, and success.

Your Spacecraft

We are not all the voices we hear in our heads.

Most of humanity hears these same voices.

Many of these voices are beliefs and fears that have been floating around, in different languages or forms for thousands of years!

How Much are You Worth?

♥♥♥♥♥♥♥♥♥

The most important question is:

How much do you think *you* are worth?

It is all about your self-worth!

Is it time to throw off the old habits and create new empowering voices in our heads, cheering us on, as we voyage here?

We Are Running on Autopilot

Would it be okay
to take some time
to think of and
catalogue how many
of these old programmes
could be hindering
your current progress
and success?

Is it time to
reprogramme your
autopilot?

The Voices in Our Heads

You can't choose all your thoughts, but you can choose to stop the ones you don't like from nesting in your hair!

Shoo them off like you would pigeons coming to eat the newly growing seeds in your garden.

Then build a net of belief, over those freshly growing shoots to protect them from any past habitual fat birds that would seek to devour them and you.

The Fear of Change

♥♥♥♥♥♥♥♥♥

For us, there is still
the chance to throw off
the chains of fear
and conformity–to write
our own programmes.

We can start living
once again the empowered
life that is our birthright
and destiny.

Do you desire it
enough, to take the steps,
to make it happen?

Are Your Gauges of Wealth, Happiness, and Success Stuck?

Are you ready to shed past fears and limitations and take full control of your direction again? It is time to fill up with *love*, pour on some deep abiding *joy*, and let loose some extra *happiness*, without the worry about those who would consider you insane!

Let's rip out all thoughts of conformity and fly.

The fulfilment of your desires and intentions is just around the corner from abandoned old beliefs and habits.

Are You Making Your Own Decisions?

**The ultimate choice
and responsibility
is given to us,
in how we control
and fly our craft.**

**It's time to seize
control back from
the autopilot and the
programmes of others,
and fly back to love!**

**You are the pilot!
You have the *power*!
Seize the day!**

Do You Believe That You Can Fly?

♥♥♥♥♥♥♥♥♥

Never fear though, as it is always possible to get the craft flying again!

Write some new programmes, replace the fuel, and take off towards your destiny. We are designed to fly high! It just takes some adjustment of that autopilot, refuelling with good, clean and fresh fuel, a bit of retraining, and we can all be on our exciting flight back to *Love* and loving every moment.

Do You Believe That You Can Fly?

The majesty of choice
is ours!
I firmly believe
there is no dream
that can enter
the heart of man,
without Spirit
or Love,
also being able
to make a way
to help us fulfil it.

We Are Meaning Making Machines!

♥♥♥♥♥♥♥♥♥

Whenever anything happens to us, thoughts usually come up and go into activity to search for a meaning or reason; and also, often to look for where to place the blame.

Do everything you can to avoid placing blame!

Taking personal responsibility for every event is one of the first steps to finding new directions and flying back to *Love*.

We Are Meaning Making Machines!

Let's set a guard
over the meanings
we make and then accept.

Let's see, even if it's tough,
that we can find the place to
believe that 'Life Loves Us' and
everything that happens is
unfolding in perfection.

These beliefs sure make for a
less ruffled, more confident and
peaceful journey.

Be Aware! Your Fears Can Create Your Next Reality

**The crazy thing is
that almost
none of the fears
we experience
are real,
or will ever
come to pass!**

**Thoughts,
if repeated enough,
will tend to become
the realities of
the imagination
in which we dwell.**

Be Aware! Your Fears Can Create Your Next Reality

After all which would you really prefer: a life full of the manifestations of your fears; or if you could, would you rather choose a life painted with the bright colours, heavenly sounds, and the ecstatic feelings of your choice?

**Take some time now
to dream, visualise, and
create a story
full of the feelings of,
and the outcomes,
that you would really like.**

Be Aware! Your Fears Can Create Your Next Reality

**Know that between the clouds,
and always above the clouds,
the sun ever shines.**

**Even during the worst and
darkest night of the soul,
the sun is just on the other side
of your planet, speeding
towards a new sunrise.**

**A fresh, purified,
and rested you will soon be
welcoming a new day!**

**Hang in there;
there is always a rainbow
to be found after a storm, and in
the belief 'Life Loves Me.'**

Letting Go

♥♥♥♥♥♥♥♥♥

I believe we are all blessed
with the power of choice
and when we believe this,
'All things are possible.'

Sometimes though,
when we get stuck in our ruts,
it is difficult to see above them.

The ruts of fear and stuck
programming have often created
deep pits where a helping hand
or permission to rise
above the mire of life's
problems can be a great help.

This can be all it takes to be
propelled out of those ruts
and overcome.

Love or Fear, Your Choice

♥♥♥♥♥♥♥♥♥

There exist only two states:
***Love* or *fear*.**

When we can stand
as an observer, take a deep
breath of clarity and see
which of these realms the
thoughts that are bombarding
our consciousness
are emanating from,
then we have the power
to accept and embrace,
or let them go,
and shun them.

Love or Fear, Your Choice

♥♥♥♥♥♥♥♥♥

It could be
as easy as choosing
to face the light,
rather than facing
into the darkness.

When we face
into the light,
all we can see is light
and that wonderful light
melts the darkness,
which then flees of itself.

Just believe!

Love or Fear, Your Choice

♥♥♥♥♥♥♥♥♥

**Remember there is
a core place within,
where no matter what is
happening on the outside,
everything is okay.**

**It's that magical part
of you that will live forever,
and cannot be touched
by any of life's storms
and disasters,
and also,
can never die!**

What Is Disease?

**We know that
our outer world
is created by
or through
the manifestation
of our thoughts
and feelings.**

**As these solidify
into beliefs,
they create
our experiences.**

**There is also a time lag, so it
is the thoughts of yesterday,
that we are living in today.**

What Is Disease?

Change your thoughts!

Change your life!

**What thoughts,
affirmations
and actions could you
incorporate into your
habitual patterns
that would now
serve you?**

How would you like to feel?

What Is Disease?

When you receive your miracle and the transformation of thought, be sure not to grab those old thoughts again.

They never were you or yours, until you took ownership of them.

They are only disempowering or negative energies, which are meant to just keep on flowing by.

Stuck Energy Can Move Again!

Many modern miracles of healing have been accomplished just by a change of belief.

Much of what controls our smooth flights, is to do with our beliefs and attitudes.

Correct them by whatever means possible and your spacecraft will be healed and well on its journey back to Love.

Stop Beating Yourself Up!

'There is no such thing as failure!'

Failure is just a bad way to view the seemingly unpleasant events of life!

Are you in the middle of a perceived failure?

If you can, take a step up, or into the secret place of your heart and then look down on the bigger picture.

Failure or Another Disguised Step Forward?

Without seeming disappointments or temporarily perceived failures, that next phase of growth, through change, could never have occurred!

There is a wonderful promise you can claim.

'All things work together for good, to those who Love.'

No Is Almost Never Personal!

Only Love can melt any lurking fears and insecurities.

Is what's holding you back the fear of being told 'No', which most of us grew up with, as an almost staple diet?

Let's journey back and show some kindness and love to that hurt inner child, understanding where we are coming from, in the realisation that we, too, have committed the same actions with others and whoever hurt us was also a victim of their own world experiences.

No Is Almost Never Personal!

**In our core, in energy,
and essence,
we are all Love!**

It just remains for us to pass through all the processes and experiences of this journey, to purify and cleanse us again.

**We will all, in time,
return to that pure state of being, leaving behind all past sad experiences and fears like old clothes, dirty and torn.**

No Is Almost Never Personal!

Let us return again
to the powerful truth that
'Life Loves Us.'

I am convinced
that when we
have all got tired
of the many games
and illusions
of this journey,
we are all destined
to return
to that place
and Being of
Unlimited Love.

What Are You Looking For and What Do You Notice?

**Pause, take some
deep breaths and decide:
is this experience
what you really
want to focus on?**

**Then make your choice
and fly your craft
back into the sunshine.**

**Our journey here is too short
to mar it with the weights,
which the person who may have
committed such an atrocity,
will never feel anyway!**

Improve It! Don't Attempt to Fix It!

We have all
been programmed
to look for
what is wrong,
and then figure out
how we can fix it.

Remember though,
what we focus on expands,
so if not checked,
our whole experience
could soon be
full of things
needing fixing!

Improve It! Don't Attempt to Fix It!

Make a list
of what is working
for you,
dwell on it for a while,
and then cement
its effect with a generous
coating of gratitude.

Repeat the process
a few times a day
for several days
and then take stock
of how your mood
and feelings have lifted.

Working Your Way to Heaven Won't Work!

**Love is the solution,
becoming childlike again
in the simplicity of Love;
the uplifting of Joy
with childlike faith
and gratitude;
that is Life itself,
which has bestowed
the greatest gift
of the being,
of a priceless part
of Divinity,
on each part
of itself,
which is Us.**

Shit Happens!

♥♥♥♥♥♥♥♥♥

When we go through life and are presented with learning experiences, with the potential to extract lessons, and potentially growing in understanding, the shit comes out.

Why do we sometimes choose to wallow in it for days and often, at that time, decide these are bad experiences?

How much better could we feel, if we chose to believe and programme ourselves that these were empowering growth experiences.

Hold On! The Crown, the Fruit, and the Rewards Are On Their Way!

**It's amazing how often,
after that seeming defeat,
followed by that tenacious
human tendency to stick it out,
there comes great victory.**

**It seems that a part of
our growing process is
the testing of our resolve.**

**That testing often comes
before the universe can
reward us with our ultimate
desires and blessings.**

Hold On! The Crown, the Fruit, and the Rewards Are On Their Way!

♥♥♥♥♥♥♥♥♥

Can you see it?
Have you heard it?
Do you feel it?

The next time you are tested, look deep within; call out for the resolve, and hold on for that wonderful victory—it is there waiting to bless your faith.

The inbuilt power of the life within can carry you through to every victory and the ultimate fulfilment of your desires, purpose, and destiny.

Take Responsibility!

How about if we reprogrammed our spacecraft with the belief, that we are in some way responsible for everything that happens in our lives?

That is, every result, each situation, and especially our attitudes and the meanings we take from each experience.

Could this help our flight levels of success, happiness, and the direction we are flying in?

Ask How

♥♥♥♥♥♥♥♥♥

Do you need the answer to some deep question?

Use the Law of Attraction.

Get quiet and from the centre of your deep desire and beautiful heart, sincerely ask the magic question: How?

Then listen and watch in quietness and confidence—without presupposition, without impatience—and the answer will almost always be there or be arriving soon, sometimes in the most magical of ways.

Ask How

♥♥♥♥♥♥♥♥♥

Mission Control for the space fleet is in most cases in great radio communication, and looking to answer our questions or send a supply craft with our needs.

It's just that sometimes we are a little further away from the centre and it can take a bit longer, or there is a temporary electric storm of those fears and disbelief disrupting communications; or maybe, just for a while, we are passing on the dark side of the moon.

What Does It Take to Become Free?

First, realise
that not all the voices
and beliefs are yours,
or empowering your voyage,
or letting you travel
where you may want to go.

I'd suggest
a deep soul searching,
and then taking time
to write down the thoughts
from the voices you hear
and the beliefs
that are at the forefront
or even in the depths
of your being.

What Does It Take to Become Free?

**The great thing
about beliefs
is they are not true!**

**They are just
accumulated thoughts,
repeated time
and time again
until they become
the strong chords
and habits that
frequently restrict
our actions
and beings.**

What Does It Take to Become Free?

What would you like to believe?

Believe it or not, you can choose!

Wouldn't it be so much more powerful to craft a series of your own beliefs, which can help you fly in the directions of your choice and experience the fullness of your desires?

Two Things That Will Crash Your Spacecraft

Judgement is
a terrible thing!

In comparing ourselves
with others, we are either
lifting ourselves up in
self-righteousness and
puffing up our ego—which
doesn't need it—or we are
demeaning ourselves
and therefore sealing
our place in a morass
of low self-esteem
and failing
self-confidence.

Two Things That Will Crash Your Spacecraft

**We will find
that life flows
so much more smoothly
when we look
at each other as equals,
looking for
the best in people
and situations—not how
we are better
or worse than
them—but realising
we have much to learn
from everyone
that crosses our path.**

Two Things That Will Crash Your Spacecraft

There comes a point
in life where
if we are to grow,
we must take control of
and abandon many
of the old ways,
and base emotions
that we were taught,
or had adopted
as a part of mankind's
early fight for survival.

There is no way to
'Fly Back to Love'
if we are still carrying
the burdens and
weights of the past.

Two Things That Will Crash Your Spacecraft

**Forgiveness, even
if a tough pill,
is the key
to healing
and to a life
once again
flowing in harmony.**

**If needed, take that step
and you will soon see
how your spirit and
emotions will lift—just from
shedding the weights
that have previously
held you back.**

Two Enemies of a Smooth Ride, in the Right Now

Let's take a look at the two biggest destroyers and enemies of peace, joy and happiness.

They are remorse over the past and fear about the future.

Let go! **Look for ways to change your focus, guard against, and root out from what could be the beautiful garden of your mind any seeds of those repeating thoughts that seek to keep you looking backwards instead of looking at today in wonder and gratitude.**

Two Enemies of a Smooth Ride, in the Right Now

Focus now
and take the time
to think about
what you really
would like.

It is much more
productive and
has the power
to take you
on your voyage
to far better places.

Two Enemies of a Smooth Ride, in the Right Now

So what about the *now*?

Yes, right now!

What if we could just be here?

Which we are, anyway!

So let's focus on this moment, with presence and gratitude, with our eyes wide open to its wonders, its beauty, its promise and its potential. It is the birthing place of all things and the crucible of creation, which can—if we just let it—lift our vibrations into higher spheres of experience and abiding joys.

What do You Fill and Program Your World With?

Why would you
want to spend
so much
of your time,
watching
other people
getting wealthy,
playing out their
or your dreams,
when you could
be playing out
your own dreams
in the blockbuster
of your life?

What do You Fill and Program Your World With?

**We are
what we eat,
and we become
like all
we associate
with!**

**Let's be fully aware
and choose wisely,
all the things
and actions
that create
our worlds.**

Be Careful What You Focus On!

**Do you think
about what
you really want?**

**Or do those
stray thoughts,
which float by,
start to build
new realities
of their own
in your world—
before you are
fully aware of
what they
are creating?**

Be Careful What You Focus On!

♥♥♥♥♥♥♥♥♥

**Be aware,
thoughts become
and create things!**

**We are creation machines
and we often don't realise
the powers we are
wielding—they shape
the world we live in!**

**Our thoughts, mixed
with the energy
of emotions, become
our intentions, which, in turn
become our manifestations.**

Be Careful What You Focus On!

Now all changes come from decisions and sometimes it can be just as simple as that.

The miracle is the change of heart or direction.

In other cases where everything seems completely overpowering, is it time to ask *Love* for the power and help to change things?

Sincere Heart Cry, Can Change Your World

♥♥♥♥♥♥♥♥♥

It is all about the change of our perception or beliefs.

**The miracle is
that magic moment
when the darkness flees;
when we turn
back to the light,
and once again
can focus on
all that is Love
and light.**

**Then the miracle
is free to manifest.**

Sincere Heart Cry, Can Change Your World

**Whatever the trial,
whatever the dark
situation is for you,
know that deep
within—in that secret
place—there is always
an answer
waiting for you.**

**Your tears of surrender
and heart cry,
if needed,
can always find it!**

Change Is Just One Heartbeat Away . . . But?

Which would you like first: the good news or the bad news?

The good news: change happens in a heartbeat.

The bad news: it usually takes commitment, effort, and determination to make it stick.

Change Is Just One Heartbeat Away . . . But?

**When your desire
to change is mixed
with belief and
some skills and actions,
it then becomes
greater than the
inertia of the old
habits, programmes,
and beliefs.**

**Then that marvellous
change can happen
in a heartbeat!**

Change Is Just One Heartbeat Away . . . But?

**Change happens
in a heartbeat;
and desire
with absolute
commitment; and
no looking back
can cement it
into your
new reality.**

There is an Ancient Practice That Can Change Your World

Take a look at your thoughts from the centre of your being.

Realise they are not you or yours, but thoughts that have swirled around this universe for years.

Shine the light of your truth on them. Are they real or imaginary?

Remember, there only exists Love or fear.

Be the observer. Let go and fly by those thoughts that don't serve the Love you are.

No More Trying Just Do It!

♥♥♥♥♥♥♥♥♥

The words we think and use all have meaning.

'Trying' would be on the bottom of any level of commitment and its use is normally an excuse, and is just plain setting ourselves up for failure.

Let's put our brain in gear before we let meaningless words flow out of our mouths and half-hearted actions dilute our effectiveness.

Why Shouldn't We?

There are too many 'shoulds' running through our heads.

In fact, most of us have been *shoulded* all over!

It is time for a change! Whether it is the voice of our parents, the rules of proper society, or our moral conscience that is screaming in our inner ears, most time a 'should' comes flying at us, it is time to duck and take a look at its compunction.

Let's find out what we really want, rather than letting the 'shoulds' blind programming push us into action.

The Power of Prayer

Rather than just continually asking for stuff, let's use our sharpened intention or prayers to create change and work miracles in our lives and that of others.

The Power of Prayer

**Thoughts are things,
and thought energy
sent with *Love*,
which is God,
is probably the most
powerful force in our world.**

**Magnify that power,
when two or more are agreed and
sending that energy together
mixed with belief,
and miracles must ensue.**

**Prayer or intention can change
personal outcomes and
even the course of nations!**

Choose Empowering Beliefs

Beliefs are neither true or false.

They just are a collection of thoughts that have been thought so many times, they have become real to us.

Choose your thoughts!

Choose your feelings!

Choose Empowering Beliefs

Some of the most basic barometers of how we feel and live our lives appear to work on set points.

Just like the thermostat's temperature setting in our homes—once set, our levels of income, happiness, wealth and health— generally come back to the points that we are comfortable with, or that we have been programmed to accept.

It's Time to Take Action! But How?

♥♥♥♥♥♥♥♥♥

From Louise Hay and Robert Holden's '*Life Loves You*' to Brian Tracey's suggestion to kiss the mirror and repeatedly say, 'I love you', the message and solutions are clear.

It is time to reprogramme your spacecraft's very vocal warning and protection systems with a different set of empowering messages.

Take Action Anyway!

**Are you too afraid
of the consequences
of the wrong choice?**

We are here to experience!

**As many wise men have
said, there is no such thing
as failure, only lessons
learnt on the journey.**

**Even realising that was not the
best choice, and learning what
you don't want, can be useful
information and a good lesson.**

What Holds Us in the Darkness?

♥♥♥♥♥♥♥♥♥

**We are, at core,
all perfect beings.**

**Our task is not
to become
perfect beings,
it is to remember
or wake up to
that fact, and shed
the cocoon of fears,
false beliefs,
and the clinging to
the identity of
our bitter experiences.**

What Holds Us in the Darkness?

The sunlight was
always there.

The promise
or inner being
of the butterfly
was always there.

It just had to pass
through the dark night
and the struggle
of the ending of the old,
into the birth of the new.

What Needs to be Shed to Bring Us into the Light?

**Our temporal world
of illusion is made up of
our beliefs, fears,
and the habits
we have accumulated,
inherited or grabbed
and clung on to.**

What Needs to be Shed to Bring Us into the Light?

Recognise life loves us.

Recognise, remember,
and repeat,
'I am Love itself.'

Do this until it becomes
an unshakeable truth
within your being.

We must let go of the fears,
lies, and false beliefs
of inadequacy
that keep us in
the worlds of darkness.

The Law of Attraction

♥♥♥♥♥♥♥♥♥

What we focus on expands!

**Strangely, this is why
many people say
'*The Secret*' and
the Law of Attraction
don't work.**

**We often spend too long
thinking about, or worse yet,
talking about what we
don't want—thus, as
what we focus on expands,
what we don't want will quickly
be on its way into our reality.**

The Law of Attraction

If you want to
change your world,
focus on what you'd like
and the qualities
and things
that you desire.

Just trust,
have faith,
and know deep inside,
all you desire is,
in due course,
on its way!

Empowerment

♥♥♥♥♥♥♥♥♥

**I am convinced
if we believe
that there are helpers,
and the anointing
to help with any task!**

**We can be empowered
to accomplish
almost anything!**

What Will You Wear Today?

**A great way to
start the day
would be with a smile,
an empowering thought,
a little laugh,
and a quick dose
of gratitude.**

**You can choose,
but for a phenomenal day,
I'd suggest that practice,
either before,
or just after
you open your eyes.**

What Will You Wear Today?

♥♥♥♥♥♥♥♥♥

Our emotions
are like clothes.

We can choose
what we wear!

They are not us,
or an integral part
of our core being;
they are choices
we make
that maybe
have become habits.

What Will You Wear Today?

Would you choose,
the bright vibrant
colours of love,
joy and compassion
to be glowing
with happiness
that can melt
and change your world,
touching hearts
and inspiring,
lifting your own spirit
and all the people you meet?

The Mystery of Money

**Money is not
a piece of paper!**

**It is almost just a value
that we give ourselves,
though it is much more!**

**It's also the value
we give things
ours, or others.**

**They say:
'Calculate your net worth'.**

**What a terrible way
to value yourself!**

The Mystery of Money

**Money, like everything
else, is energy!**

**It almost doesn't exist
in our physical plane,
yet we can feel it,
or especially we can feel it,
when we perceive or believe
that we don't have any,
or can't get it; especially when
that burning emptiness,
desire, or desperation kicks in,
when we feel we don't have
enough for something
we need or want.**

The Mystery of Money

I'd suggest
the best way
to treat money
is like a sensitive lover
or a gentle dove.

Don't hold it too tight
or it will be gone!

Don't lock it away
and withhold it,
or it will be of no use.

It, like energy,
works best and
prospers most in flow.

Have You Found Your Golden Goose?

In all your endeavours, remember the Golden Rule.

Whatever you do, do it in *Love* and with consideration for others—Win-Win!

Then the Dream and Goal, the Holy Grail of Financial Freedom, will be on its way. You will find it is worth all the growth, labour and testing you will experience en route to that achievement.

The Pursuit of Happiness

First—just maybe
learning to be happy
in whatever state we are in
could bring the start of a
higher and more fulfilling way.

Then all things and wisdom
could be free to help us
to really take off and fly
in this wondrous
playground of life.

Could it be all it takes,
is to realise
how wonderfully wealthy
we already are?

The Pursuit of Happiness

**Happiness is not something
we just get by actions
or possessions,
but something we choose!**

**Our happiness level
can be full, regardless
of exterior situations.**

**Like the old question,
which comes first: the chicken
or the egg?**

**I'd say happiness comes first,
and then we can experience
the golden eggs of life.**

Sex, Nudity, Freedom, and the Divine

♥♥♥♥♥♥♥♥♥

**The opportunity
for heavenly bliss
and connection
is inbuilt,
yet in so many cases,
we have been sold short
and end up
with a quick spurt
of limited sensation.**

Sex, Nudity, Freedom, and the Divine

Set your boundaries and live with them, but be careful they don't become chains that destroy the experiences and pleasures that are a part of the functions of our incredible crafts.

Especially, make sure that they are the boundaries of your choice, and not some arbitrary blockages programmed by others for a different age or situation and held in by the fears and the penalties thus imposed.

Sex, Nudity, Freedom, and the Divine

♥♥♥♥♥♥♥♥♥

It was the Divine
that created
your beautiful body
and filled it
with so many
pleasure sensors
that it's almost
impossible to count them.

So enjoy it, and
all the pleasures
and love it can bring.

Life Loves You!

Forgiveness Is Loving Ourselves!

It has been said that
forgiveness is the perfume
a beautiful flower leaves
on the heel that crushed it.

Consider that gift of forgiveness.

It is a blessing,
in spite of all the hurt,
which has to come
from a source far greater
than our human ego!

I believe each of us has
that place of Divine love within
and can, if we choose, reach it.

Forgiveness Is Loving Ourselves!

♥♥♥♥♥♥♥♥♥

Take some time in the beauty
of your heart that special place
of Love, where all forgiveness
of self and others flows—bathe
in its balm, enjoy the perfume
of a thousand flowers
that can be found there;
relax, let all past hurts
be washed and cleansed
with the powerful prayer.

'I'm sorry, please forgive me.
Thank you, I love you.'

Are You Planning Your Life?

First, believe that you can and then take some time out and decide what kind of life would be your ideal?

Consider if money and time were not limiting, what would you like to do, to be and to have?

If you believe it and invest time in creating it in your heart and thoughts, 'All things are possible to him or her that believes.'

Don't be afraid to dream!

The master plan for our voyage here, it is for our enjoyment, not drudgery, poverty and pain, or even just shades of the same.

Past Lives or Seeing Through the Eyes of Others that Have Been Before?

**The collective being,
which is the mind,
energy and spirit
that empowers us all,
has observed many
human experiences
throughout the ages
of this earth.**

**Was it actually us
or me that experienced
these events?**

Do You Desire a Soul Mate?

This is a huge desire
burning in the hearts
of many alone
or lonely people.

Sometimes, this pull is
stronger and at other times,
walls and protections have
been built against it, often
caused by previously
wounded hearts.

Yet so frequently,
there remains a calling
deep in the heart
that desire for a special
intimate connection.

Do You Desire a Soul Mate?

The journey is not
just about the tough
moments of growth
it can be,
most especially,
about the
many beautiful
moments of connection,
empathy, and the
shared pleasures
of *Love* creating
and *Love* making.

Some Tips and Ideas Experienced from My Soul Mate Manifestation Process

It is not all about finding the perfect soul mate; in fact, he or she will be just as imperfect as you believe you are. So how about looking to become more like the one that your ideal soul mate would desire?

Yes, make your list of what you would like in your soul mate, though realise the journey and the quest can often be more about realising what you don't like.

Some Tips and Ideas Experienced from My Soul Mate Manifestation Process

**The most important step
in finding and keeping the *Love*
and in fact everything you desire
is to *Love* yourself!**

**So working through
that journey, clearing and
cleansing all self-hating
and limiting beliefs,
is the prime step
in finding and keeping
all the experiences
you desire.**

Integrity—Live in Truth

♥♥♥♥♥♥♥♥♥

Strangely, integrity isn't only about how we treat others.

One of the worst people you can lie to or let down is yourself—after all, you have to live with yourself 24/7!

If we are in inner conflict and lacking in self-respect or self-love, we will have already been defeated in all genuine attempts to win hearts and influence others and live a life of integrity.

People sense our own feelings about ourselves and they treat us accordingly.

Integrity—Live in Truth

It takes
creating time
for growth, and also
consistent practice
and concerted effort
to continue in
the right direction.

However, the miracle
of a change of thought,
which can be
just a decision,
is all that is needed
to make a start.

I Am

**Take a look at your life
and see how many
'I Am's'
it would benefit
you to replace?**

**Use what you
desire to become,
and not the
limiting thoughts
that you may
have been
imprisoning
yourself in.**

For Those Suffering Loss

♥♥♥♥♥♥♥♥♥

Know that,
though it seems
realms away,
through walls created by
forgetfulness and senses
almost lost in the past
the place where we all abide
is only a thin veil away.

In that special place,
that quiet place
in the temple of your heart,
you can connect
through that veil
and know all is well.

For Those Suffering Loss

There can be beauty even in great loss and new beginnings. Life is waiting to show you its smile—when you are ready to receive it.

Take a look. The sun always eventually comes out from behind the dark storm clouds. That storm having washed and cleansed the earth.

What new life would you like to create?

Believe everything and anything is possible.

Healing can be in a moment.

Reaching Your Idea of Heaven Is Not the Goal It's Enjoying the Journey!

Too many of us fly
through life, chasing the
elusive butterfly of success.

The trouble is that we never
catch it, or even if it appears
we do for a few seconds,
then it's soon off again.

We eventually burn out
ourselves, and also often those
closest to us—that is if they
didn't flee a long time before.

Reaching Your Idea of Heaven Is Not the Goal It's Enjoying the Journey!

In our relentless pursuit of
success, it's too easy to forget
what life is really about!

Surely, it's the collection of our
experiences and the memorable
moments that count!

Remembering too,
Love and happiness
gauges that measure full
most of the time—no matter what
the circumstances or situation
we find ourselves in.

An Adventure in Goal Setting

**Before any journey
as in life,
there comes a time
when we must decide
where we want to go,
or what we want
to achieve.**

**Unless we have a purpose
and a reason that some call
our 'Why', which helps us
set a direction,
then our life frequently
just drifts in mediocrity.**

An Adventure in Goal Setting

**Have you decided on or
taken time to listen to Spirit
and discover your purpose?**

**Have you laid some plans,
the course, and direction
for how you can attain
this grand vision
or souls calling?**

It's never too late!

An Adventure in Goal Setting

♥♥♥♥♥♥♥♥♥

You are never too old,
or too young,
and there are almost no limits
to the diversity of goals,
desires, and dreams
that can be attained.

It just takes that desire,
mixed with energy
and direction,
and the willingness
to blast off,
leave the comfortable
earth behind and fly
towards your dreams.

Have You Created a Vision Board?

Avoid wanting things too much, as this becomes almost a dwelling on the lack of them.

It is the intention of desire and the knowing, that they are there already in your confident future that your treasured desires have already been created and are just awaiting the perfect time for you to step into them.

This is what brings them smoothly into being!

Have You Created a Vision Board?

When you have done
all of the smaller steps
to prepare, create in thought,
and be ready,
then the Universe
and your Higher Self
will see you mean business,
and the flow will begin.

The treasures
of your tomorrow
are waiting to be created
in your beautiful heart
and thoughts today.

How Do You See the World?

I'm convinced
that we all have choices
and what we choose
to visualise and see,
in time, creates our reality.

We can choose to live
in routine mediocrity
or create through thoughts
and our beliefs—which are
merely repeated thoughts
our dream worlds.

How Do You See the World?

♥♥♥♥♥♥♥♥♥

If we can believe
and live our vision,
with passion
and persistence,
in spite of all
the world throws
at us,
what changes
may be accomplished
and hearts won!

The Ramblings of a Mad Man

Most pioneers, visionaries, world changers and prophets, have at first been considered insane by the masses—at least until their invention, discovery, or warning became manifest.

Their completely different lifestyles, ideas and results have explored places that normal people would fear to go.

To hell with the proper way!

Perfect Peace in the Midst of a Storm

♥♥♥♥♥♥♥♥♥

Once we turn in the light of that great truth and face the Light of Love—throwing ourselves into its warmth and caring shelter—nothing can harm or steal the peace it can bring.

It is once again down to the inner belief that '*Life Loves Me.*'

Find that within or through the wonderful exercises of mirror work, meditation, and other modalities.

Then, even the most terrible storms of this life will never be able to steal your knowing and inner peace.

Perfect Peace in the Midst of a Storm

♥♥♥♥♥♥♥♥♥

Face the light.

Let nothing turn your gaze.

The miracle of
the transformation of thought
from fear into love is there.

It is ready to manifest
its eternal peace.

Nothing can harm or destroy
the *Loving* energy that is you!

The Tapestry of Life

**When everything
seems like
it is going wrong,
when failure
and discouragement
is on every side,
think of this story
and remember:**

'Life Loves You!'

The Tapestry of Life

♥♥♥♥♥♥♥♥♥

In spite of all her fears and self-doubt her creation was now finished in its perfection and beauty.

If only they could all see everything that had gone into the making and the story of this beautiful work.

How often do we lose the vision of all that is being created and accomplished through our labours of love?

The Mystery of the Temples and Life

♥♥♥♥♥♥♥♥♥

Feel the power of that life within.

And know that the whole of you is pulsing with the vibrations of the entire cosmos that nothing can destroy, the energy of that Love itself—which continues long after the earthly vehicle and the illusion, even of a physical temple, has crumbled into the death of the ages.

Look deep inside.

Connect with that Eternal Being, which is You and Life itself—and Live.

Death – The Ultimate Journey

♥♥♥♥♥♥♥♥♥

**At core,
we are love,
which is energy.**

**Even science teaches that
'energy cannot be destroyed,
it can only change form!'**

**So death, or better labelled
'passing'—a finishing of this
earthly journey, is just the time
when the core or soul energy
of our being is parted
from its spacecraft and
returns to source.**

Death – The Ultimate Journey

♥♥♥♥♥♥♥♥♥

It has been said
that death is like sleeping
and we shall all wake up.

I have a feeling that
it's actually us on this voyage
that are more in that sleep state.

Most people have forgotten
the truths about the reality
of our beings—but not the 'dead'
who are once again
in a timeless state
and have already woken up.

Death – The Ultimate Journey

♥♥♥♥♥♥♥♥♥

Let us shed every fear
and thus be free again
and ease all the burdens
of loss and despair.

We can then rejoice when
our dear ones have parted,
with the knowledge
of their and our eternal beings,
dancing together again
in the wonders of forever.

If truth were known,
we are all one,
and never parted anyway!

Void, Nothingness, or a Place of Loving Energy?

For me a life of Love,
being, and experiencing
all the wonders
it can create and enjoy
that seems to be
a great purpose
and a Divine calling.

I'm just curious,
what kind of forever
would you like to live?

You Never Lose by Giving

♥♥♥♥♥♥♥♥♥

Now there is
a balance in this,
as some have given so much
there may be nothing,
or almost nothing left to give.

Self love is such
an important lesson,
giving to oneself,
taking time to recharge
and being filled with Love
in that special place within.

You Never Lose by Giving

♥♥♥♥♥♥♥♥♥

It is important to give out of love, for giving out of duty, or by being too full of the idea of personal gain, or from a place of resentment or bitterness, instead of true love surely has no reward.

Like with everything, when we move away from Love, there is only cold darkness left. Sadly, it seems our modern world has become a very selfish place.

The values of Love and giving are frequently lost in the quick fix of personal gain and instant gratification.

All You Need Is Love

♥♥♥♥♥♥♥♥♥

We can't see love,
or can we?

We can feel its warmth
in a smile and see its effects
and the changes
created by its energy.

It can warm a life
and melt the hardest heart.

Yet often we isolate
ourselves against it
in fear of being hurt
or being consumed
by all the changes
it can bring.

All You Need Is Love

The only law in creation
is to Love,
as some would say;
'God's only Law is Love!'

How we play out
these earthly roles
now and in the
illusions of pasts
and futures are of
no significant consequence
to the greatest truth
that we are, and I am,
the loving energy
that comprises
all things!

Where Are You Choosing to Live?

♥♥♥♥♥♥♥♥♥

There can be a period
of awakening or realisation
of different core beliefs,
values, and realm of being.

This is where
we are becoming aware
of our true nature
that heavenly being,
in our earthly spaceship
on a journey of experience,
growth, and pleasure
in this temporal illusionary
earthly domain.

Where Are You Choosing to Live?

**When that shift is complete,
I can dip in and out of life's
wonderful experiences,
enjoying all its pleasures
and sensory thrills,
confident in the powerful
knowledge that
I am living in Love.**

**Then I know that nothing can hurt
or destroy in that Holy Mountain.**

**I am living life in a far
more real realm, in the knowledge
of the powerful spirit that
I am, and we are.**

Index

Thank You!

If you got this far I trust you enjoyed the book.

If so please visit and like it at:

www.facebook.com/TheLittleBookofLove.info

Also please visit the Books website at:

www.TheLittleBookofLove.info

See the last page also for information on the parent book, "Take Control of Your Spacecraft and Fly Back to Love." All these quotes are wrapped with much more detail, information and solutions in its pages.

About the Author

♥♥♥♥♥♥♥♥♥

Keith Higgs has lived an interesting and exceptional life.

A hippie search for truth; twenty years of International Christian-based voluntary work; Editing and publishing talks and inspirational audios; Building a successful computer business—then watching it crash; Two marriages, eight children and six stepchildren; Building a MLM business, Learning from the masters of personal growth; Attending and assisting at talks and workshops; Studying NLP, healing and speaking skills; Building a social media platforms of thousands; Travelling many countries.

His combined skills, common sense, learnings and accumulated wisdom have flowed into '*Take Control of Your Spacecraft and Fly Back to Love - a Manual and Guidebook for Life's Journey.*'

Here is a man who has lived and learnt. He has a passion to share his truths, values, and beliefs with many.

Contact Keith for Speaking or Workshop Bookings

Website: www.KeithHiggs.com

Email: Keith@FlyBactoLove.com

Facebook: www.facebook.com/KeithHiggs1

To Get Your Copy, Read or Listen to the Full Book or to get the eBook.

Visit www.FlyBacktoLove.com

A free explorer membership of the interactive website is available or Copies can be purchased there or through Amazon, Audible or any good bookshop.

Lightning Source UK Ltd.
Milton Keynes UK
UKHW021045050321
379837UK00016B/2205